D1455866

GRASSHOPPERS

by Mary Ann McDonald

The Child's World

Content Adviser:
Jeffrey Hahn,
Department of Entomology,
University of Minnesota

Published in the United States of America by The Child's World®
PO Box 326 • Chanhassen, MN 55317-0326
800-599-READ • www.childsworld.com

PHOTO CREDITS

© Anthony Bannister; Gallo Images/Corbis: 11
© Bill Beatty/Visuals Unlimited: 18
© Gary Meszaros/Dembinsky Photo Associates: cover, 1
© Jim Richardson/Corbis: 26–27
© Ken Preston-Mafham/Animals Animals-Earth Scenes: 24–25
© Mary Ann McDonald/Corbis: 5
© Maximilian Weinzierl/Alamy: 14–15
© Patrick Robert/Sygma/Corbis: 22–23
© Patti Murray/Animals Animals-Earth Scenes: 7, 16
© Robert & Linda Mitchell: 9, 21
© Stephen Dalton/ Animals Animals-Earth Scenes: 28–29
© Tom Murray: 12–13

ACKNOWLEDGMENTS

The Child's World®: Mary Berendes, Publishing Director;
Katherine Stevenson, Editor

The Design Lab: Kathleen Petelinsek, Design and Page Production

LIBRARY OF CONGRESS CATALOGING-IN-PUBLICATION DATA

McDonald, Mary Ann.
  Grasshoppers / by Mary Ann McDonald.
    p. cm. — (New naturebooks)
  Includes bibliographical references and index.
  ISBN 1-59296-639-X (library bound : alk. paper)
  1. Grasshoppers—Juvenile literature. I. Title. II. Series.
  QL508.A2M186 2006
  595.7'26—dc22   2006001367

Table of Contents

On the cover: This lubber grasshopper is resting on a green leaf. These grasshoppers are common in the southern United States.

Meet the Grasshopper!

Grasshoppers have been around for about 245 million years.

On a sunny summer day, you go walking in a grassy field. The tall grass is waving in the breeze, and birds are calling in the distance. Suddenly, you see a bug jump in the grass nearby. You look in that direction, but you can't see where the bug went. You take a few steps forward, and the bug jumps again. This time it lands on a nearby flower. You bend down for a closer look and see a small creature with long, backward-pointing legs. What could this creature be? It's a grasshopper!

Differential grasshoppers like this one are very common all across North America. They grow to be a little less than 2 inches (5 cm) long. You can find them in fields, woods, and even along the edges of ponds and lakes.

What Are Grasshoppers?

Adult grasshoppers grow to be about one to five inches (3 to 13 cm) long.

A grasshopper can leap 20 times its body length.

Grasshoppers have five eyes. They have one large eye on each side of their head, and three smaller eyes between them.

Grasshoppers are a kind of **insect**. Insects have bodies with three parts—a head, a middle section (called the **thorax**), and a tail end (called the **abdomen**). Insects also have six legs and either one or two pairs of wings.

Grasshoppers have two pairs of wings—a sturdy pair near the front of their body, and a large, thin pair near the back. Grasshoppers use their wings to make short glides from place to place. And while grasshoppers are good gliders, they are even better jumpers. Their back legs are long and specially made for leaping. The ends of the legs have little hooks to provide a strong grip.

This lubber grasshopper is resting on a plant in Florida's Everglades National Park. "Lubber" is another word for a clumsy person. Lubber grasshoppers got their name because they are slower and clumsier than other grasshoppers.

Are There Different Kinds of Grasshoppers?

Grasshoppers have their eardrums on the sides of their abdomens. Crickets and katydids have their eardrums on their front knees.

There are many different kinds, or **species**, of grasshoppers, and they come in many different shapes, colors, and sizes. All grasshoppers have feelers, called **antennae**, on their heads. Grasshoppers touch things with their antennae to learn about their surroundings. Grasshoppers have short antennae, while related insects (such as katydids and crickets) have longer ones.

Grasshoppers live in almost every area of the world. In fact, everywhere there are plants, there are grasshoppers! Some grasshoppers like moist, dark areas, while others prefer hotter, drier places. The most popular **habitats** for grasshoppers, however, are grasslands, meadows, and woodlands—places where there are lots of plants to eat and places to hide.

Here you can see this barber-pole grasshopper's sensitive antennae. These grasshoppers live in the southwestern United States.

How Do Grasshoppers Make Noise?

Only male grasshoppers make noise.

When insects make sounds by rubbing their legs, it's called *stridulation* (strih-juh-LAY-shun).

Male grasshoppers are some of the best singers in the insect world. They "sing" by scraping one body part against another. One of the body parts, called the *file,* has hard ridges. The other, called the *scraper,* has a sharp edge. Rubbing the file across the scraper makes a loud sound. Different kinds of grasshoppers make different sounds. They also have different "songs" for calling females, challenging other males, and sounding an alarm.

Here you can see the inside of an orange-winged grasshopper's leg. The file is on the blue part of the leg. The scraper is on the grasshopper's front wings.

File

Grasshoppers have their files on their back legs. Their scrapers are on the edges of their front wings. To make chirping sounds, they rub one of their legs over a wing. Grasshopper relatives (crickets and katydids) have both their files and their scrapers on their front wings. They make noise by raising their wings into the air and rubbing them back and forth. The band-winged grasshopper even makes a sound when it flies! It snaps its wings and makes a crackling sound as it flies through the air.

When flying insects make sounds with their wings, it's called *crepitation* (creh-puh-TAY-shun).

Band-winged grasshoppers like this one are common in desert areas with short grasses. The crackling sound they make comes from their brightly colored hind wings.

13

How Are Baby Grasshoppers Born?

Grasshopper eggs are about the size of a grain of rice.

Depending on the species, egg groups contain 15 to 150 eggs.

The male grasshopper "sings" to attract a female. After they mate, the female lays eggs through a special egg-laying tube called an **ovipositor**. Most grasshoppers have a short ovipositor. They use it to dig a hole in the ground. Then they lay their eggs in clumps at the bottom of the hole. A few grasshoppers (and all katydids and crickets) have longer, curved ovipositors. They use their ovipositors to slit open plants and then lay their eggs inside.

This female locust is using her ovipositor to lay her eggs in the desert soil.

14

When grasshopper eggs hatch, baby insects crawl out. These babies, called **nymphs**, look like adults, only much smaller. But unlike adults, the nymphs cannot glide. It takes several months for each nymph to grow into an adult. During that time, the nymph eats plants to grow bigger and stronger.

The first nymph to hatch in a group leaves a tunnel in the dirt as it makes its way to the surface. The nymphs that hatch after it have a much easier time—they just climb through the already-made tunnel.

These lubber grasshopper nymphs are resting on a bush in Florida. Compare these nymphs with the adult lubber shown on page 7.

17

When you grow, so does your skin—but the skin on a grasshopper nymph does not. Instead, as the nymph gets bigger, it must **molt**, or shed its outer layer of skin. When the old skin gets too small, it splits down the back, and the nymph pushes its way out. A newer, bigger skin is waiting underneath.

As they molt, grasshoppers gulp air to build up pressure in their bodies. The pressure helps them split their old skins.

Newly hatched nymphs are white. After a few hours in the sunlight, their colors and markings darken.

Here you can see a green-striped grasshopper nymph next to its older skin. Like all newly molted nymphs, this one is holding still while its new skin dries. After a few hours, the nymph will hop away to find something to eat.

What Do Grasshoppers Eat?

Locusts can be very destructive. Sometimes they gather in huge groups, called *swarms*, and eat fields full of crops.

Grasshoppers' droppings, like those of most insects, are called *frass*.

Grasshoppers are **herbivores**, or plant-eaters. They spend almost all of their time eating—and sometimes they eat every leaf, blade of grass, or vegetable in sight! The mouthparts of grasshoppers are made for biting and chewing. Sometimes even clothing and screen doors aren't safe from hungry grasshoppers.

This bird grasshopper is eating a blade of grass in Texas. You can see how some of the grasshopper's mouthparts hold the food while other parts chew.

Are Grasshoppers Pests?

The Turnbull grasshopper is said to be a help to farmers rather than a pest. This grasshopper eats plants such as goldenrod and thistles—which farmers consider to be weeds.

Grasshoppers and their relatives have damaged more crops and other plants than any other animal in history. Sometimes billions of grasshoppers get together in huge swarms. Then they jump and glide over hundreds of miles of land, eating all the plants in their path.

This swarm of desert locusts has taken over a tree in Algeria.

How Do Grasshoppers Stay Safe?

Some grass-hoppers spit a brown liquid when threatened. The grasshopper on page 11 left some of its liquid on the photographer's finger.

Grasshoppers have many enemies. Birds and other animals think grasshoppers make tasty meals. Many grasshoppers depend on their coloring to hide them from enemies. This coloring, called **camouflage**, helps grasshoppers blend into the leaves and grasses around them. Sometimes an enemy will be right on top of a well-camouflaged grasshopper and not be able to see it!

Other grasshoppers escape danger by jumping or gliding away, showing their brightly colored wings as they flee. This sudden burst of color confuses the enemy and gives the grasshoppers extra time to get away. The lubber grasshopper uses a different kind of protection. When frightened, it oozes a stinky foam from its mouth and body! This foam helps keep other animals at a distance.

Foaming grasshoppers like this one live in South Africa. The foam these grasshoppers give off tastes terrible to anything that tries to eat them.

How Can You Study Grasshoppers?

Some types of grasshoppers change colors with the seasons. They are green in the spring and summer and change to red or brown later in the year. This helps them stay camouflaged as the plant colors change.

During the summertime, it's easy to study grasshoppers. You can walk into a meadow or field and sweep the grass with a large butterfly net. You might even catch several different kinds. If you have an insect book, you can try to find out what kinds they are before you let them go.

Can you guess what type of grasshopper this boy is watching? Here's a hint: the same species appears on page 7.

We often think of grasshoppers and their relatives as pests, but they also are fascinating creatures. They are also a natural part of the world around us. So the next time you are hiking through a sunny meadow, keep your eye out for leaping grasshoppers. Stop for a moment and listen. Can you recognize the grasshoppers' songs?

There are two other important differences between grasshoppers and crickets. First, grasshoppers can glide, while crickets can't. Second, grasshoppers are active during the daytime, while crickets are active mainly at night.

Here is a close-up look at a meadow grasshopper as it jumps from a leaf. Can you see how its legs move backward to push the grasshopper into the air?

Glossary

abdomen (AB-duh-men) The abdomen is the belly area of an insect. Grasshoppers have a skinny abdomen.

antennae (an-TEH-nee) Antennae are the feelers on an insect's head. Grasshoppers use their antennae to touch and learn about the world around them.

camouflage (KAM-uh-flazh) Camouflage is coloring that lets animals blend in with whatever is around them. Many grasshoppers use camouflage to hide from enemies.

habitats (HA-bih-tats) Animals' habitats are the types of surroundings in which the animals live. Grasshoppers live in many different habitats, especially grasslands, meadows, and woodlands.

herbivores (HERB-ih-vorz) Herbivores are animals that only eat plants. Grasshoppers are herbivores.

insect (IN-sekt) Insects are animals that have six legs and a body divided into three main parts. Grasshoppers are insects.

molt (MOLT) When an insect molts, it sheds its old, outgrown skin. Grasshopper nymphs molt several times before they become adults.

nymph (NIMF) A baby insect is called a nymph. A grasshopper nymph looks like a little adult grasshopper.

ovipositor (oh-vih-PAHZ-ih-tur) An ovipositor is a special egg-laying tube that some insects have. Grasshoppers have ovipositors.

thorax (THOR-aks) The chest area of an insect is called its thorax. Grasshoppers have a thorax.

To Find Out More

Read It!

Allen, Judy, and Tudor Humphries (illustrator). *Are You a Grasshopper?* New York: Kingfisher, 2002.

Dallinger, Jane. *Grasshoppers.* Minneapolis, MN: Lerner, 1981.

Harman, Amanda. *Grasshoppers.* Danbury, CT: Grolier Educational, 2001.

Pascoe, Elaine, and Dwight Kuhn (photographer). *Crickets and Grasshoppers.* Woodbridge, CT: Blackbirch Press, 1999.

Poole, Amy Lowry. *The Ant and the Grasshopper.* New York: Holiday House, 2000.

Squire, Ann O. *Crickets and Grasshoppers.* New York: Children's Press, 2003.

On the Web

Visit our home page for lots of links about grasshoppers:
http://www.childsworld.com/links

Note to Parents, Teachers, and Librarians: We routinely check our Web links to make sure they're safe, active sites—so encourage your readers to check them out!

31

Index

About the Author

Mary Ann McDonald is a professional wildlife photographer (she took the picture on page 5) who lives in central Pennsylvania with her husband Joe, also a photographer and writer. She has photographed wildlife around the world, from Rwanda to Chile to Yellowstone National Park. Mary Ann and Joe teach photography workshops at their home, which they call Hoot Hollow. Mary Ann's photographs have appeared in many national and international publications, including Ranger Rick, Your Big Back Yard *and* National Geographic Kids.